# The Merry Christmas Activity B❄❄k

## Jane Bull

DK Publishing, Inc.

LONDON, NEW YORK, MUNICH,
MELBOURNE, and DELHI

DESIGN • Jane Bull
EDITOR • Penelope Arlon
PHOTOGRAPHY • Andy Crawford
DESIGNER • Sadie Thomas

PUBLISHING MANAGER • Sue Leonard
MANAGING ART EDITOR • Clare Shedden
PRODUCTION • Alison Lenane
DTP DESIGNER • Almudena Díaz

For Grandad
Freddie

First American Edition, 2005

Published in the United States by
DK Publishing, Inc.
375 Hudson Street
New York, New York 10014

05 06 07 08 09   10 9 8 7 6 5 4 3 2 1

A Cataloging-in-Publication record for this book is
available from the Library of Congress.

ISBN: 0-7566-1369-8

Color reproduction by
GRB Editrice S.r.l., Verona, Italy
Printed and bound in Italy by L.E.G.O.

Discover more at
**www.dk.com**

Have some frosty, festive fun

# Make a merry Christmas . . .

## Sprinkle sparkly greetings . . .

## . . . and cook up some gifts

# Glittery greetings

## Pour on the glitter

and send a Christmas card
with added sparkle to your
special friends.

4

**Get out your glitter**
Gather up all the sparkly
things you can find:
Glitter • Glitter glue pens
Sequins • Jiggly eyes • Stickers
Gift ribbons • Tinsel
You'll also need posterboard,
a paintbrush, and some white glue.

# Conjure up a glitter card

Paint-brush

White glue

Fold a piece of posterboard in half.

**Paint your design with glue.**

**Sprinkle on the glitter.**

...ut down a sheet ...f newspaper ...o catch the ...litter.

**Shake it off.**

...nish your card ...ith extra ...ecorations, ...ch as stickers ... paint.

Don't waste any!

Fold the newspaper in half.

Pour the glitter back.

Any shape cutter will work.

white glue

Dip a cutter in glue, press it on the paper, then cover it with glitter.

8

# Special gifts

## Wrap and tag

Dip it, print it, wrap it, tag it! It's great to give gifts but even better to give them wrapped in homemade paper complete with matching tags.

9

# How to print....

**Clear a space,** you are now going to do some big printing! Find some plain paper that is big enough to wrap presents in—a roll of brown shipping paper is good—and get printing. Remember to do an extra stencil that you can cut out and turn into a matching tag.

## Frosty the potato man

Cut a potato in half, dab it in the paint, and press the potato onto the paper. Repeat for the body shape.

### You will need:

• Sheets of plain paper
• Sponges
• Odds and ends to print with
• Acrylic paint
• Cardboard for the stencils
• Pen and scissors
• Ribbon or string to attach the tag

## Shooting star stencils

Draw a star on a piece of paper.

Cut out the star.

Place the stencil on your wrapping paper. Dip the sponge into some paint and dab it over the stencil.

Take the stencil off carefully— you don't want the paint to smudge.

# Spongy festive forest

Draw your shape on a sponge.

Cut it out.

Glue the sponge onto a piece of cardboard.

Now print your trees onto the wrapping paper and decorate them with red and gold paint.

## Pen-cap printing

Pen caps make pretty patterns.

Use the base of your pen to make a big circle.

Try using the eraser at the end of your pencil.

## Camouflage kit

Print with a scrunched-up plastic bag to make it look like camouflage.

# Snowy bunting

## Deck your walls
with flurries of snowflakes and streamers of happy snowmen.

# How to make snowy bunting

**The trick** with this bunting is to take a piece of string, then thread your decorations onto it with a straw between each one to separate them. Try these simple ideas.

OLD GREETING CARDS

........ Take some old cards and cut them into shapes.

STRAWS

STRING

Punch a hole in the paper snow.

## Paper snow

Turn to page 47 for instructions on how to make snowflakes, and string them up for a flurry of festive fun.

SINGLE HOLE PUNCH

LOTS OF PAPER SNOW SHAPES

## Paper plate flakes

Now make colorful snowflakes and attach them to paper plates, or turn the plates into smiling snowmen.

HOLE PUNCH

SCISSORS

GLUE STICK

STRAWS

STRING

PAPER PLATES

PAPER SNOW

PAPER

Cut the snowman's face out of paper or posterboard and glue it on.

Glue the paper snow onto the plates.

14

# Snowy greetings

Don't throw them out! Last year's greetings cards make instant colorful decorations. Cut the cards into shapes, punch a hole in them, and string them up with straws in between to separate them.

Thread the snowflakes on the string with straws between them.

STRAWS

STRING

Thread string through the straws and the holes in the plates.

Remember to knot the ends so everything stays on.

Punch holes in the plates.

15

# Baubles,

## ...stars, and 3D trees

Make them small to hang on a tree

or huge to hang from the ceiling,

but whatever you do, hang them up!

16

## 3D trees

For a 3D look, slot two shapes together. Try two circles as well, to give a bauble effect.

**1.** Cut two tree shapes exactly the same.

Cut a slot in one tree from the top to halfway down.

**2.** Now cut a slot in the other tree.

Cut up from base to halfway up.

**3.** Slide one shape onto the other.

**4.** Stand your tree up, or stick on some thread and hang on the tree.

## Paper baubles

If you use old, recycled Christmas cards, all the decorations will be completely different. You could also use your homemade printed paper.

### Little or large

String me up and hang me up

# How to make baubles and stars

## For baubles you will need

Old greeting cards • Thick paper • Ruler • Pen • Scissors •
Hole punch • Paper fasteners • Thread

### Paper baubles

REUSE OLD
GREETING CARDS

RULER

PENCIL

SCISSORS

**1** Cut the card into strips

SINGLE HOLE
PUNCH

Punch the holes
at the bottom
and the top.

**2** Punch holes

Tie thread around
the paper fastener
to hang it up.

Clip
the strips
together at the
bottom and the top.

PAPER FASTENERS

**3** Clip together

**4** Fan out the strips to form a ball

# Super stars

**You will need:**
Paper • Pen • Scissors • Thread • Tape

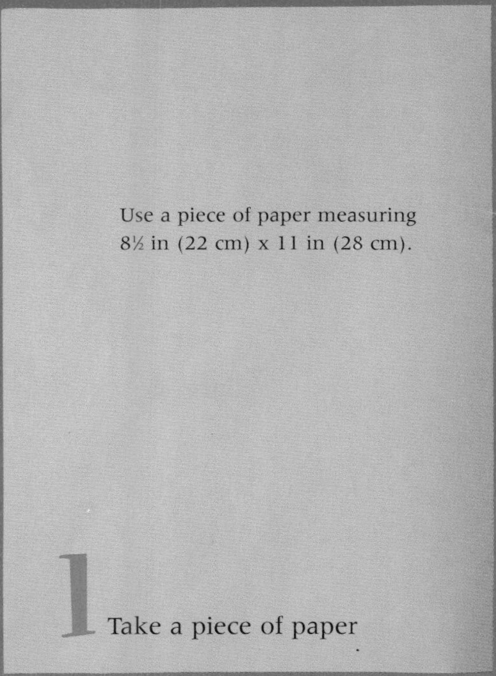

Use a piece of paper measuring
8½ in (22 cm) x 11 in (28 cm).

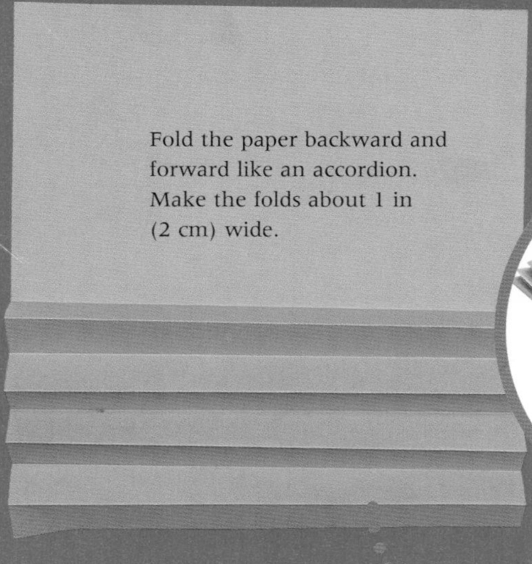

Fold the paper backward and
forward like an accordion.
Make the folds about 1 in
(2 cm) wide.

Fold the
folded paper
in half.

**1** Take a piece of paper

**2** Fold into pleats

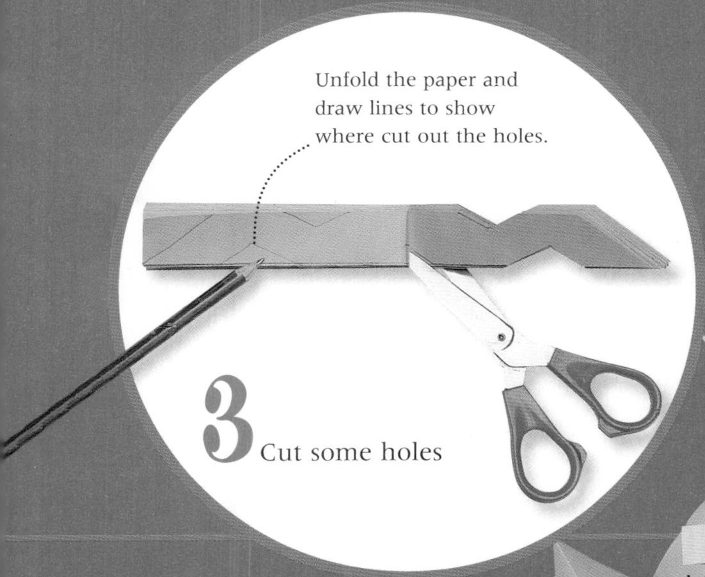

Unfold the paper and
draw lines to show
where cut out the holes.

Fan out the paper
and tape the sides
together.

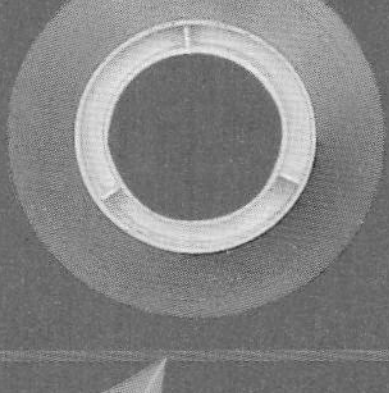

**3** Cut some holes

**4** Tape the edge

Tape the other side to
complete the circle,
then add a piece of
string to hang it up.

**5** It's a star

# Christmas night
### Hush now, all is quiet.
Light your lanterns and watch them twinkle in the dark to welcome festive friends.

# Four decorative designs

When the candle burns, it can reveal a host of angels, colorful spots, stained-glass shapes, or a starlit skyscape. All you need is a jelly jar and tissue paper.

Alternatively, glue tissue-paper circles onto your tracing paper.

**3** Tissue paper

Cut out some blue tissue paper the same size as the tracing paper, draw stars, and cut them out.

**2** Cut out a landscape from colored paper and glue it to the tracing paper.

**4** Glue the blue paper to the back of the tracing paper.

Festive forest

**1** Cut some tracing paper to fit around a jar.

**5** Wrap the sheet around the jar.

Tape in position.

# Shining star jar

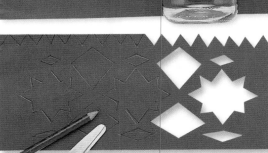

**1** Cut a piece of paper the height of the jar and long enough to fit around it.

**2** Snip a zigzag along the top and draw and cut a pattern out of the middle.

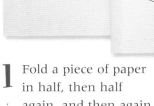

**3** Glue a different-colored piece of tissue paper to the back of the design and wrap the paper around the jar.

# Glowing angels

Draw a design on the folded paper, and cut it out.

**1** Fold a piece of paper in half, then half again, and then again.

**2** Unfold the paper.

**3** Make the paper into a crown shape and tape the ends together. Slip it over a large jar.

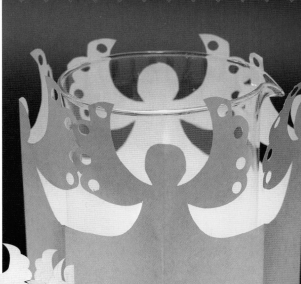

This design slips over a jar—it's not attached like the others.

23

# Festive windows

**Day and night**, give your room a Christmassy glow
with these tissue paper windows

**1**

SCISSORS

PENCIL

Draw your picture on a sheet of
dark-colored posterboard, and cut
out some shapes.

**2**

Glue pieces
of tissue to
the back of
the picture.

GLUE
STICK

**3** Turn your picture
back over.

COLORED
TISSUE PAPER

Now stick your silhouette
in the window and let
it shine out!

24

# Clever cutouts

Instead of a picture, try cutting out a snowflake from folded paper. Turn to page 47 to find out how to make one.

*A flurry of snowflake windows.*

# Winter woollies

Soft and squashy felt decorations hang around with fuzzy pompoms.

# How to stitch some woollies

**Collect some colorful felts** and threads. Cut out two shapes, sew them up using blanket stitch, stuff them with something soft, and decorate with sparkly sequins. Turn to page 46 to make pompoms.

NEEDLE-THREADER

GOLD OR SILVER THREAD

LOTS OF DIFFERENT COLORED FELT

SEQUINS AND RIBBONS FOR DECORATION

WHITE GLUE

PINS

## Needles and pins

You will need:
• embroidery needles (use a needle-threader to help you thread a needle)
• Glue
• Stuffing

COLORED EMBROIDERY FLOSS OR THIN YARN

POLYFILL

SCISSORS

## Cutting shapes

Turn to page 48 to find the shape templates.

Cover the page with a piece of tracing paper.

Trace over the shapes with a pencil.

Glue a heart to the triangle shape.

### Angels and fairies

# Cut out, stitch, and stuff

Pin your template onto a piece of folded felt and cut it out.

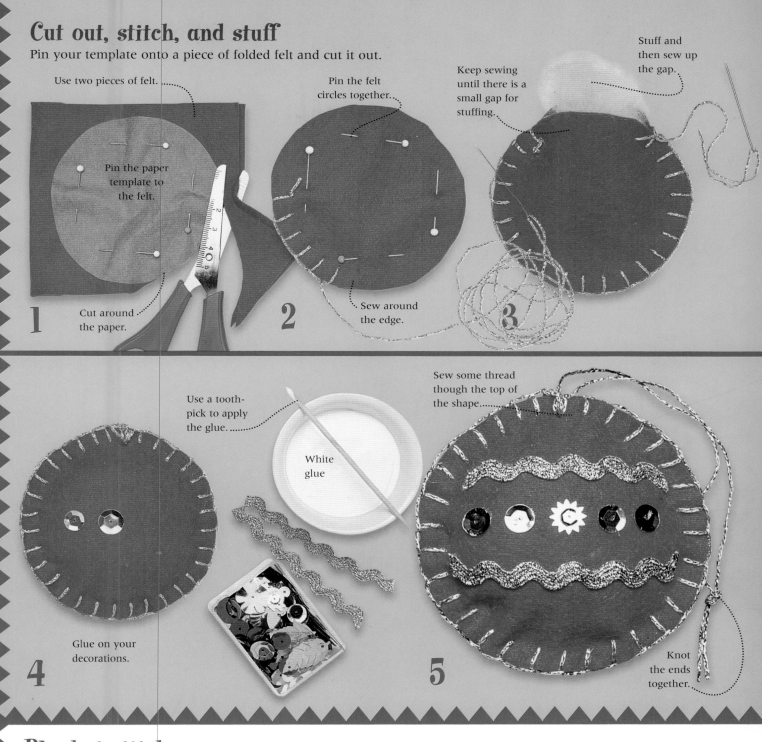

Use two pieces of felt.

Pin the paper template to the felt.

Cut around the paper.

**1**

Pin the felt circles together.

Sew around the edge.

**2**

Keep sewing until there is a small gap for stuffing.

Stuff and then sew up the gap.

**3**

Use a toothpick to apply the glue.

White glue

Sew some thread though the top of the shape.

Glue on your decorations.

**4**

Knot the ends together.

**5**

# Blanket stitch
This stitch looks great and is easy to do, but keep it neat!

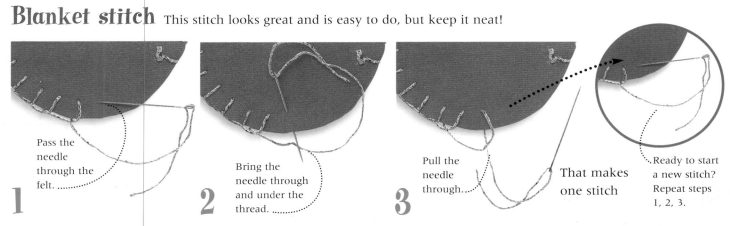

Pass the needle through the felt.

**1**

Bring the needle through and under the thread.

**2**

Pull the needle through...

**3**

That makes one stitch

Ready to start a new stitch? Repeat steps 1, 2, 3.

# Christmas scents

**Sweet and spicy** mixes of cinnamon and cloves with the fruity aroma of orange fill the air.

Pomanders and potpourri—perfect to give as presents.

# Making scents

**Rich, spicy smells** are all around at Christmas time, so why not gather them up and bottle them?

Pour in the ingredients

## Mix up a pot of scents

To make potpourri, spoon spices, such as ground nutmeg and mixed spice, into a jar. Then add cinnamon sticks, nutmegs, cloves, etc. to fill it. Turn the jar over to mix it up and keep it in a cool, dry place. Keep turning it once a day for four weeks.

Put on the lid.

Turn the jar each day.

Keep turning for weeks.

CINNAMON STICKS

WHOLE NUTMEGS

ALLSPICE BERRIES

ORRIS ROOT

MIXED SPICE

STAR ANISE

# Clove-studded oranges

These scented fruits are called pomanders. Oranges work best, but you could try other citrus fruits, too. The jeweled pomander will last only a few days, but the clove-studded orange will last for much longer.

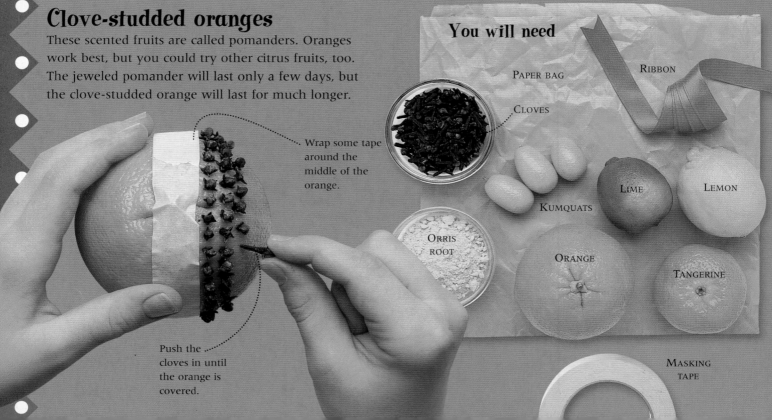

## You will need

Wrap some tape around the middle of the orange.

Push the cloves in until the orange is covered.

PAPER BAG

RIBBON

CLOVES

LIME

LEMON

KUMQUATS

ORRIS ROOT

ORANGE

TANGERINE

MASKING TAPE

GROUND NUTMEG

GROUND CINNAMON

Cinnamon sticks

PINE CONES

WHOLE CLOVES

After about six weeks, your potpourri will be ready.

## Some scent tips

POTPOURRI • Because the ingredients are dry, it will last forever, but the scent will fade after a few months.

POMANDERS • As the orange dries out, it will shrink and only the cloves will show. It will smell nice for weeks.

ORRIS ROOT • You can buy this in health food stores. It's used to help preserve the sweet smells.

Glass-headed pins and sequins.

Jeweled pomander

Mix up the pins and the cloves for a colorful, jeweled look.

Put the orris root into a bowl.

Wrap the orange in a paper bag.

Remove the tape and tie it up with a ribbon.

Roll the orange around until it is coated.

Tape up the top.

Leave in a warm, dry place for six weeks.

33

# Sugar and spice

Yum Yum

**Spicy cookies**
With a hint of orange, dipped in sweet icing.

35

# Mix up some spice

**Stir up the spice**—these delicious cookies can be served up right away or can be stored in an airtight jar or tin for a few weeks.

ASK AN ADULT to help with the oven.

Set the oven to 375°F (190°C)

Sugar

Butter

Mix them together to a creamy mixture.

## 1 Cream together

Add all the ingredients.

Flour

Orange rind

Cinnamon

Ginger

## 2 Add the flavor

## 3 Mix it all up

Squeeze the mixture into a ball.

Wrap the ball in a plastic bag and put in the refrigerator for two hours.

## 4 Make a ball

Sprinkle some flour on the table.

Cut the ball in half.

Roll out the dough to ¼ in (5 mm) thick.

Cut out some shapes.

## 5 Roll it out

Make holes for ribbons with a straw.

Place the shapes on a cookie sheet.

Put in the oven and bake for 15 minutes.

## 6 Shape and bake

# You will need:

¾ CUP BUTTER

½ CUP BROWN SUGAR

1⅔ CUPS FLOUR

2 TEASPOONS GINGER

2 TEASPOONS CINNAMON

GRATED ORANGE RIND

## 7 Now decorate

Remove them from the oven and put them on a rack to cool.

Sugar and water icing

When the cookies are cold, decorate them with icing. Mix 3 tablespoons of confectioner's sugar and 3 teaspoons of water. Decorate with dragées, or any tasty decorations that you like.

Spoon on the icing and smooth it out.

## Make a snowman cookie

Cookie cutters

Cut two circles.

Join together.

Decorate

# Secret snowman

## Surprise, surprise! What's Frosty hiding under his hat?

# Secret snowballs

They're not just a pretty decoration to hang on the tree, but a secret stash of goodies. Give one to a friend and fill it with gifts.

Pull your snowball apart...

...and let the goodies roll out

Off with his hat!

Look what's inside...

# Make a paper pot

WHITE GLUE

BALLOONS

TORN-UP NEWSPAPER

To stop the paper from sticking to the balloon, spread petroleum jelly on it.

**1** Cover the balloon with white glue.

**2** Spread pieces of newspaper over the balloon, leaving the bottom uncovered.

**3** Repeat steps 1 and 2 six more times. Finish with a layer of white glue.

**4** Leave it to dry for a day or two.

Use a jar to support it.

*Pop!*

When it's hard and dry, pop the balloon.

# Make a secret snowman

You will need to start with two pots the same size. That means you will have to blow up your balloons to match. One will be for the hat and the other for the head.

**2**

HAT    HEAD

*Trim them down*

**1**

The dotted lines show where to trim them down.

*First make two pots*

## Paint and PVA

Mix equal amounts of paint with PVA (white) glue. This gives a nice sheen when dry and makes the pot stronger.

FOLD ALONG DOTTED LINES

## Nose template

Trace this nose shape and cut it out of card.

**3**

MASKING TAPE

Wrap it in masking tape.

Scrunch up some paper into a ball.

Use a strong glue to fix it in place...

### Trim the hat

**4**

Stick on a folded paper nose with strong glue.

Paste some pieces of paper over the seams.

### Add a nose

**5**

Paint them with white paint mixed with white glue.

Leave them to dry.

### Paint them all white

**6**

Mix the paints with white glue.

### Give him a face

## Make a bauble

Make two pots and this time blow up two smaller balloons to the same size.

**1** Make two small pots.

**2** Trim them down.

Cover with white paint.

BASE POT          POT LID

**3** **Ask an adult** to make a small hole in the bottom of each pot.

**4** Decorate the pots with paint and glitter.

**5** Take a piece of ribbon 22 in (60 cm) long and tie the two ends together.

Pass the ribbon up through the hole in the large pot.

Push the ribbon through the hole in the lid and now you can hang it up.

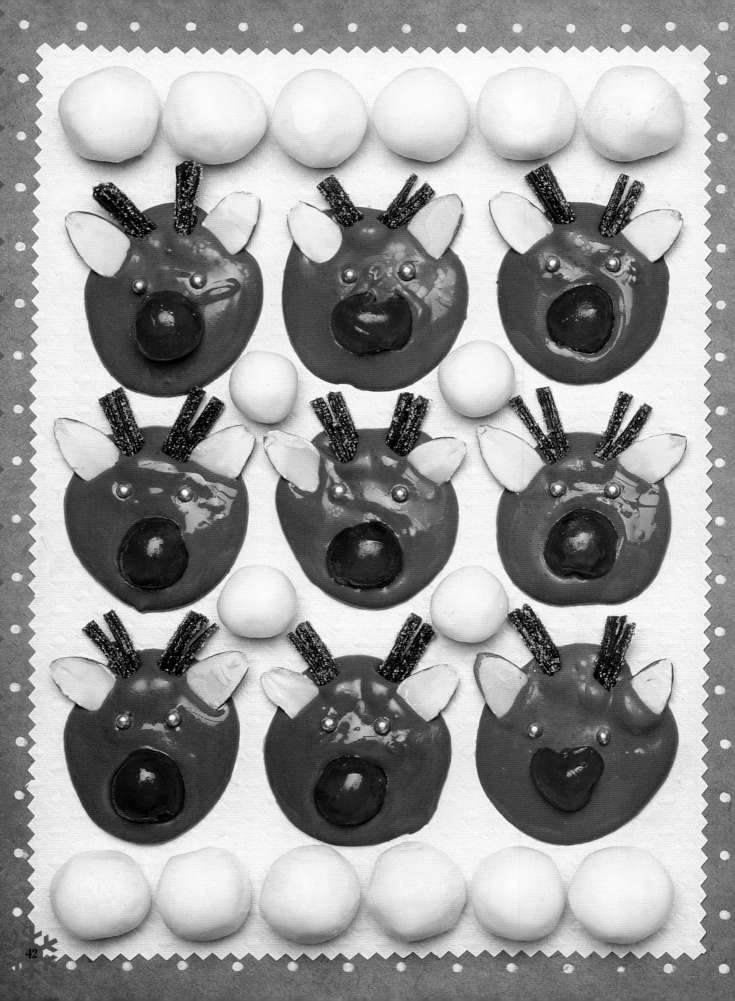

# Sweets and treats

**Dig in** to minty snowballs and Rudolph chocolates all laid out on a plate, or wrap them up sweetly to give away as tasty gifts . . .

yum yum!

## Chocolate Rudolphs

You will need:

ALMOND HALVES

CANDIED CHERRY HALVES

JELLY CANDY STRIPS

SILVER DRAGÉES

CHOCOLATE 6 OZ (170 G)

COOKIE SHEET AND WAX PAPER

## Minty snowballs

PEPPERMINT EXTRACT

You will need:

ONE EGG WHITE

3½ CUPS POWDERED SUGAR

COOKIE SHEET AND WAX PAPER

# Making sweet treats

## Chocolate Rudolphs

Melt the chocolate over a bowl of hot water.

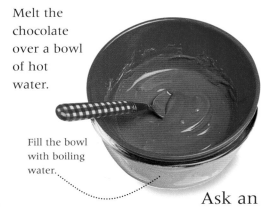

Fill the bowl with boiling water.

### Ask an adult
to help with the hot water.

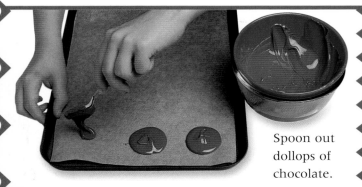

Spoon out dollops of chocolate.

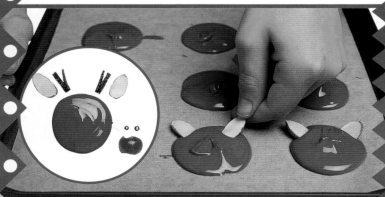

Before the chocolate sets, add Rudolph's face.

Leave them to set.

## Minty snowballs

Separate an egg.

Place an egg cup over the yolk.

Press the egg cup down firmly in place

Pour the white into another bowl.

Whisk up the egg white.

Stop whisking before the egg white gets too stiff.

Add four teaspoons of peppermint extract

Add the egg white to the sugar.

Mix it all together.          Make into a ball.

The snowballs will be the size of large marbles.

Leave them to harden overnight.

Cut up the ball.          Make some snowballs.

# Make some gifts

## Use the projects in the book to create presents for your family and friends.

....Up, up, and away

Chilly treats

Pop your cookies into an air-tight cookie jar or tin and they will last a few weeks longer.

These secret pots can hold whatever you want. Keep the snowman and bring him out year after year.

## Gifts to eat

Decorate a cookie tin and fill it with your spicy stars • A felt stocking can be be filled with goodies and hung on the tree • Wrap up some minty snowballs in a cellophane bundle • Fill the snowmen with anything you want to give away

Leave the top of the sock open....

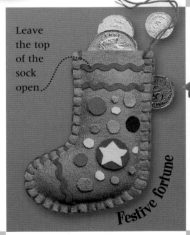

Festive fortune

Potpourri will keep its scent if sealed in a jar until it's time to give it away.

Fill felt ornaments with dried lavender and sew up as shown on page 29.

You could fill a plastic bag with your mints.

Minty bundle

Gather it up at the top and tie with a ribbon.

## Scented gifts

Decorate a jar of pot-pourri with a bright, festive ribbon • Present pomanders in pretty boxes plumped up with tissue paper or fabric and finished off with a ribbon • Stuff your felt shapes with dried lavender for a scented decoration

Remember, the more cloves you use, the longer your pomanders will last.

Pretty pomander sits in a special box....

# How to make pompoms and snowflakes

## Woolly pompom

Make some pompoms to go with your winter woollies on page 28.

**1** Cut two discs from posterboard.

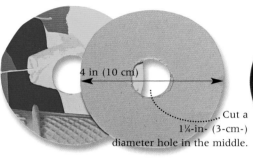

4 in (10 cm)

Cut a 1¼-in- (3-cm-) diameter hole in the middle.

**2** Put the two discs together.

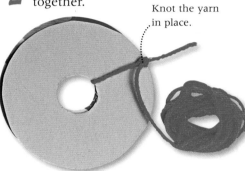

Knot the yarn in place.

**3** Wind the yarn around the discs.

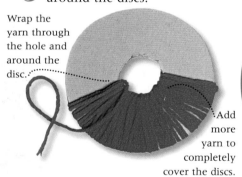

Wrap the yarn through the hole and around the disc.

Add more yarn to completely cover the discs.

**4**

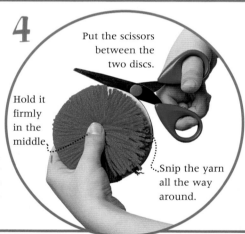

Put the scissors between the two discs.

Hold it firmly in the middle.

Snip the yarn all the way around.

**5** Open up the disc slightly.

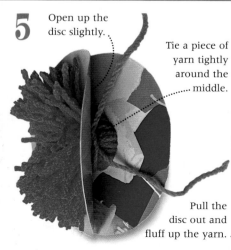

Tie a piece of yarn tightly around the middle.

Pull the disc out and fluff up the yarn.

**6**

Snip away any long bits to make a neat ball.

## Make a square

To start off your paper snowflake, it's handy to know how to make a square piece of paper.

Take a rectangular piece of paper.

Fold the top edge and line it up with one of the sides.

Cut off this piece.

Open it up and now you have a square shape.

# Paper snowflakes

Paper snowflakes can be used in many ways. Cut small ones to stick on greeting cards (page 4), medium-sized ones for festive windows (page 24), and really big ones to hang up as your bunting (page 12).

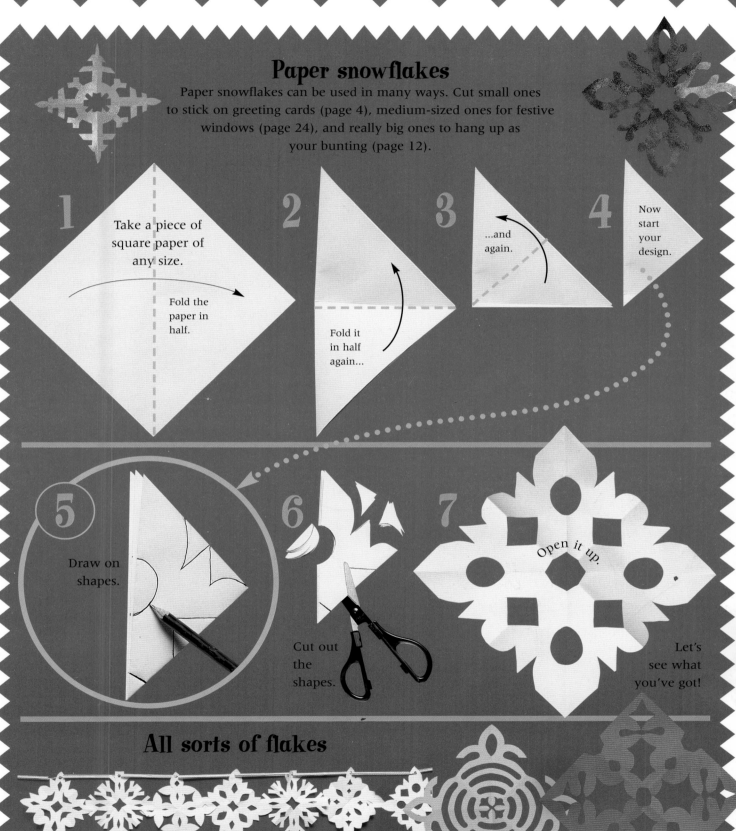

**1** Take a piece of square paper of any size.

Fold the paper in half.

**2** Fold it in half again...

**3** ...and again.

**4** Now start your design.

**5** Draw on shapes.

**6** Cut out the shapes.

**7** Open it up.

Let's see what you've got!

## All sorts of flakes

## Woolly templates

Use these templates to make the winter woollies on pages 26–29.

# Index

## Acknowledgments

With thanks to...
Billy Bull, James Bull,
Seriya Ezigwe,
Daniel Ceccarelli, Lulu Coulter,
Harry Holmstoel for being
merry models.

All images © Dorling
Kindersley.
For further information, see:
www.dkimages.com